Single Mothers and Living For Christ 2

Tréasa Brown

Copyright © 2021 by **Tréasa Brown**

All rights reserved. No part of this publication may be reproduced by any means, graphics, electronic, or mechanical, including photocopying, recording, taping, or by any information storage retrieval system without the written permission of the publisher except in the case of brief quotations embodied in critical articles and reviews.

Tréasa Brown/Rejoice Essential Publishing
PO BOX 512
Effingham, SC 29541

www.republishing.org

Unless otherwise indicated, scripture is taken from the King James Version.

Single Mothers And Living For Christ/ Tréasa Brown

ISBN-13: 978-1-952312-96-0

Library of Congress Control Number: 2021919004

Contents

PREFACE..vii

FOREWORD..x

ACKNOWLEDGEMENTS...xii

CHAPTER 1:	The Struggle (Welfare).........................1
CHAPTER 2:	The Impact On My Children................16
CHAPTER 3:	What God Requires From You................22
CHAPTER 4:	Preparing Your Heart..........................29
CHAPTER 5:	Did You Learn Your Lesson?..................39
CHAPTER 6:	Spiritual Growth................................47
CHAPTER 7:	The Lord Will Keep You Hidden!............53
CHAPTER 8:	"He's Not Your Husband!"....................59
CHAPTER 9:	Are You Willing To Try Again?...............68

CHAPTER 10:	Not Just Anybody!.................................73
CHAPTER 11:	The Best Is Yet To Come!......................83
ABOUT THE AUTHOR	91

Dedication

This book is dedicated to my Lord and Savior, Jesus Christ, who inspired me to write this book. I also would like to dedicate this book to my anointed grandmother, Missionary Hazel Lee Hughes, who was the phenomenal mother of 12 children. As well as all the anointed SINGLE mothers around the globe. Be encouraged!

Preface

This book contains delicate chapters of my life and different obstacles that I faced. Often people see the anointing on our lives, but they don't know the process. We witness to others, but we often neglect our process and what happens in between struggle and victory. This is the part that needs to be heard! There's nothing wrong with being discreet, but where's the transparency?

In this book, not only am I transparent as a single mother, but I impart encouragement and Scripture to under-gird my experience. The goal is to share my testimony with single mothers, or single women, in believing that they can learn through my story and reflect on their own current situations in life. My hope is that they will know their worth and value of who they are IN GOD! My prayer is that they will AVOID these same pitfalls and be the best woman of God they can be through Christ Jesus! This book is not to shine the light on all my flaws, but that people will know we serve a MIGHTY God who causes TRANSFORMATION and GROWTH in us, through the process!

James 5:16 declares, "Confess your faults one to another, and pray one for another, that ye may be healed. The effectual fervent prayer of the righteous man availeth much." My process wasn't pretty, but the end result as the Lord continues to take me through WILL glorify HIM! I'm grateful for what the Lord has done in my life! I told the Lord that if He would give me a platform to testify to the young women, I would tell them what I've been through. Well, this was the way the Lord decided to do it, even though I didn't see this coming.

He declared over my life that I was "Destined to be a writer, an Author..." I was amazed at the conformation that came through other men and women of God who are divine connections in my life! "Single Mothers and Living For Christ 2, just like the first, is meant to not only build up the single mothers, but encourage them in this walk with the Lord! We're NOT walking it out alone, but through HIM that gives us strength from day to day! I pray that you become empowered single mothers, by the word of God and that you embrace where you are in this season of your life!

Foreword

Single Mothers and Living For Christ 2 by Tréasa Brown is a powerful must-read. This book is the perfect addition to Single Mothers and Living For Christ because Tréasa Brown shares profound revelation on singlehood. Her transparency is refreshing and she mentors us through every page. She has a heart for God's people and doesn't want anyone to make the same mistakes, so she exposes the enemy's plans and encourages us to trust God. Tréasa Brown imparts wisdom so we can make better decisions. Through this book, we will gain a new perspective on singleness and discover our purpose in life. Tréasa Brown provides relatable insight and inspiration to trust God during hardships. Single Christian moms will be strengthened as they prepare to be a wife and wait for the man that God has for them.

Prophetess Kimberly Moses
CEO Rejoice Essential Magazine

Acknowledgements

Father, Son and Holy Ghost! Lord, You ALWAYS inspire me and have been my #1 encouragement! My first love! I would be lost without you! Thank you for not giving up on me, I'm desperate for you!

To my three beautiful children, DeVontaé, Julissa and Julius Steele, Mommy loves you! We're going to make it!

To my Mother, Hazel Hughes-Choyce, who has under-girded me, there's so much I could say about

Single Mothers and Living For Christ 2   xiii

you, but for now, I love you and thank you for ALL your prayers, you're the jewel in my life!

To my Uncle Joe, you have always been like a father figure in my life. Thank you so much! I love you!

To my Dad, Tommy Lee Brown, I love you and I'm praying for you!

To Daddy Choyce, thank you for all your support and prayers, we love you!

To my siblings, Caémeille Choyce, Tony and Tyler Brown, I love you all! We've been through a lot together, but God is going to get the GLORY out of our lives. It's our turn!

To my future husband, whoever you are, I know you'll be TAYLOR-MADE by God! As I always say, it's going to take a special person to fill those shoes. Manifest MOG, that we may do ministry together for the Kingdom! (An act of faith!)

Finally, to all those that encouraged me during the process of writing this second book, thank you so much for your support! I'm sure you know EXACTLY who you are! God bless you! Enjoy!

CHAPTER 1

The Struggle (Welfare)

One must wonder HOW to break the cycle of poverty repeated over the course of many generations. We've seen the struggles of our parents, grandparents, aunts, uncles, and so on. You must start to ask yourself, what are we doing to avoid the SAME struggles? Why do we see this same cycle in our bloodline? How can we push ourselves to do better? Where do we start?

Well, prayer is definitely a start! Not just for ourselves, but our children and our children's children. Breaking off curses and strongholds that seem to have us bound is essential. We've got to BREAK poverty off our future, in the name of Jesus!

Let's explore statistics. According to USA Facts, data shows that poverty rates for single mothers are the highest. Here's a little history. In 1960, the percentage of single mothers in poverty was at nearly 60%. By 2000, according to USA Facts, the percentages had decreased closer to 40%. Let's also look at poverty program spendings, such as Medicaid, TANF (Temporary Assistance For Needy Families), and SNAP/EBT (Nutrition Assistance Spending AKA, food stamps). In 2018, Medicaid spending was approximately $616.1 billion, TANF is at $28.7 billion. In 2019, SNAP spending reached approximately $58.5 billion. My goodness! We need a breakthrough somewhere. This is appalling and saddens my heart. It should start with us, as individuals and goes back to elevating our thinking! One must change their mentality!

Proverbs 13:22 declares, "A good man leaveth an inheritance to his children's children: and wealth of the sinner is laid up for the just." It's time to grab hold of our wealth! I'm not saying those that have government assistance don't need the help but don't stay confined! And just because someone needs a hand up doesn't mean they're any less. You've got women of God, such as myself, that are trying to utilize what the Lord has placed in our hands for a better life.

One's circumstances, such as having children early in life, can easily cause one to fall into the category of needing assistance. This is why we need to THINK before we act. One-time decisions can be VERY COSTLY just to fulfil the need for pleasure! (I just said something right there!) Welfare was not my choice, but I became a candidate after having my first child. I was 18, in public housing, and needed food stamps. This was my hand UP! Even though over the years, I had to learn about MY TRUE PROVIDER.

I remember I had a redetermination application review for my food assistance. The interviewer for my case had informed me that my assistance was delayed due to my redetermination. After hearing this, I began to think to myself how I was still receiving assistance, even though it was supposed to come to a halt? I was shocked! This, I believe, was the Lord's way of letting me know that HE ALONE was my PROVIDER, and SUSTAINER. THE SOURCE! So many people think the government IS their source. But when it shuts down or stops, then what? We know God as Jehovah-Jireh or Jehovah-Yireh, which in Hebrew means, "The Lord will provide." I KNOW HIM to be JUST that!

I can attest to certain resources not being enough for a season, but somehow, the Lord would have a ram in the bush! For example, do you really think that $617 or less is enough to pay bills, cover toiletries, and other emergency needs that you might have within a month? I'll let you calculate. The Lord stretched it and made it work! Whether you acknowledge it or not, many of us have experienced shortages, but someway, somehow, the Lord got us through it. Resources CAN FAIL at any given moment!

Around April 2020, when the pandemic hit, my internship working for Boulder County was coming to an end in the Content and Records Department. Prior to that, in March, COVID-19 hit me hard, and I lost my sense of taste and smell. It would've been selfish for me to continue to go into the office. For the sake of others, I reported it and stayed out of the office.

My work ended in March due to my symptoms. My children lost their senses as well. I filed for taxes that year, and while EVERYONE else was receiving their state and federal tax returns, I only received my state and one stimulus check. Currently, as I'm typing on May 19th, 2021, I'm still waiting, after a third 60-day notice given in the mail from the IRS. I filed back in February of 2020. (Crazy, huh?) Thank God I know WHO my source is! Anyone else would be going Coo Coo for Cocoa Puffs! It's been a really tough year financially, but the Lord amazingly has still been providing.

My Bible tells me in Hebrews 10:38, "Now the JUST SHALL LIVE BY FAITH." There's so much I could say right here, but I'll let that be enough for now. I'll never forget the prophecies spoken over my life by Prophet Fred Louis, Prophet Cedric Stanton, and Apostle WisePreach, concerning wealth! 3 different men of God that the Lord spoke through said similar things concerning wealth! Very profound! The Bible declares to us in Matthew 6:33, "But seek ye FIRST the Kingdom of God, and HIS righteousness; and all THESE THINGS shall be added unto you." For example, had I not been seeking the Lord's will, I would've never known that the Lord called me as an author for HIS GLORY! Please understand that your success is NOT built on what you do, but rather what HE DOES! You couldn't do it without Him.

The Lord has invested so much in us, but what will we do with it? Will we sit on it? Will we produce? Will we work for the Kingdom of God? Many of us are sitting on the Lord's investment. We won't move or act on what He told us to do! Before we know it, years have passed by, and we're in the same place we were 10 years ago! The devil is a liar! I come against stagnation and procrastination in the name of Jesus! I prophesy that you shall produce with your hands, in Jesus name and that what the Lord has invested in you will produce MUCH fruit!

If we followed the DIVINE instructions that the Lord spoke to us through prophecy, there would be no lack, but rather a multiplication! Blessings! We have thoughts like: "I'm not smart enough," "I'm not talented enough," and "I don't have the finances." Not only that, fear grips us, and we STOP. But what MANY don't realize is as you step out in faith, the Lord WILL PROVIDE! Let's explore an example in my life.

During the time of my FIRST book, "Single Mothers and Living for Christ, I sat at my desk for a moment. I remember hearing the Lord very clearly. I believe He said, "What are you waiting for...Turn it in!" I obeyed with haste and turned my book in. It was prophesied prior, by a friend of mine, that he saw me signing a contract. (God bless you, Brandon Johnson, it came to pass!) Glory To God! When I was offered my first contract by Prophetess Kimberly Moses to publish my FIRST book, the poverty mindset wanted to kick in. I began to think about finances and how payments would be made. But with my obedience came the blessing. The Lord provided every step of the way! See! When you take care of God's business, He will CERTAINLY take care of yours!

I began to put my time frame on the completion of my book. My thought was by the end of the year. But the Lord began to show me, not so! I made my first payment starting on June 3rd, 2020, and my last payment was August 2nd, 2020! My book was then published on August 5th, 2020! God IS ABLE!

Don't become comfortable and settle! While we receive help through different resources, it's time for God's plan. Seek the face of God and ask Him for direction. He holds the KEYS to your DESTINY the FINAL BLUEPRINT! Pursue it, in Jesus name! Don't ever get in a position where you NEVER UTILIZE what God has placed on the inside of you! Invest in your future! Many of us stay stagnant because we don't challenge ourselves IN THE THINGS OF GOD! Have you ever wondered why it's easier for us to be used by the world rather than by God? I'd rather be hired by God than the world. Why? Because the reward is EVERLASTING!

Have you noticed since COVID-19, MANY lost their businesses, which caused many to become unemployed? My, what an impact! Again, many saw the job as a source and NOT a resource. Yes, God provides resources, but when you start exalting the job above Him, He'll remind you of the source. We've got this thing twisted!

Though we are taught in society to look at our employment as a source of income, we are wrong! It's a resource, and again, not THE SOURCE! You see, a resource is defined as a stock or supply of money, materials, staff, and other ASSETS that a person or organization can draw on to function effectively. Whereas, the source is a CAUSE or starting point. The beginning or the place of origin. Don't overlook the one who provided from the beginning!

Sowing seed, tithing, and giving offerings is KEY! I've watched this work in my life, and the Lord has sustained me. Even through my seasons of drought, He made a way! (THE FAVOR OF GOD) In 1 Kings 17, I'm reminded about the Prophet Elijah and how the Lord spoke to him, that there would be neither dew nor rain for a certain amount of years! 1 Kings 17:3-4 the Lord declared to Elijah, "Get thee hence, and turn thee eastward, and hide thyself by the brook Cherith, that is before Jordan. And it shall be, that thou shalt drink of the brook; and I have COMMANDED the ravens to feed thee there. So he went and did according unto the word of the LORD: for he went and dwelt by the brook Cherith, that is before Jordan. And the ravens brought him bread and flesh in the morning, and bread and flesh in the evening; and he drank of the brook. And it came to pass after a while that the brook dried up, because there had been no rain in the land. And the word of the LORD came unto him, saying, Arise, get thee to Zarephath, which belongeth to

Zidon, and dwell there: behold, I have COMMANDED a widow woman there to SUSTAIN thee".

What's your point, woman of God? The Lord ALWAYS has a plan! I don't care what it looks like, single mothers. Someone may say, how can you give when you're already at your lowest? My response. Your FAITH! I'm learning that as a single mother, I had to ACTIVATE my faith in giving. It produces!

I didn't always like giving. To be honest, I was certainly not a sharer when it came to everyday exchanges. The same widow woman that was commanded to sustain Elijah had a test of her own! 1 Kings 17:11-13 declares, "And as she was going to fetch it, (she was asked to fetch Elijah some water in a vessel) he called to her, and said, Bring me, I pray thee, a morsel of bread in thine hand. And she said, As the LORD thy God liveth, I have NOT a cake, but a HANDFUL of meal in a barrel, and a little oil in a cruse: and, behold, I am gathering two sticks, that I may go in and dress it for me and my son, that we may eat it, and die. And Elijah said unto her, FEAR NOT; go and do as thou hast said: but make me therefore a little cake FIRST, and bring it unto me, and AFTER make for thee and for thy son." Verse 15 and

16 says, "And she went and DID according to the saying of Elijah: and SHE, and HE, and HER HOUSE, DID EAT MANY DAYS. And the barrel of meal wasted not, neither did the cruse of oil fail, according to the word of the LORD, which HE SPAKE by Elijah''. When you feel you have nothing left, the Lord will create and produce!

I'm also reminded of a woman in the Bible who gave all she had. I understand this very well! Mark 12:41-44 declares, "And Jesus sat over against the treasury, and beheld HOW the people cast money into the treasury: and many that were rich cast in much. And there came a certain poor widow, and she threw in two mites, which made a farthing. And he called unto him his disciples, and saith unto them, Verily I say unto you, That this poor widow hath cast more in, than ALL they which have cast into the treasury: For all they did cast in of their abundance; but she of her want did cast in ALL SHE HAD, EVEN ALL HER LIVING." Powerful! Do you know what it's like to give all your living? You don't know what's going to happen next. How will I get from point A-Z this month? I can attest that the Lord has sent unexpected blessings my way, sustaining the children and I. Things I NEVER asked for- I lie not!

I remember MANY times when the Lord spoke to me during the offering and told me the EXACT amount to give. He challenged me in my giving! People would confirm the EXACT amount that I was giving. It was appalling to me! There would be times where the Lord would nudge me to give when it seemed to be my last, but I gave it! Man, was that a challenge at times. But He was making me become a true giver, one that would learn to give cheerfully and sacrificially.

The Bible declares to us in 2 Corinthians 9:6-7, "But I say, He which soweth sparingly shall reap also sparingly; and he which soweth bountifully shall reap also bountifully. Every man according as he purposeth in his heart, so let him GIVE, not grudgingly, or of necessity: for God loveth a CHEERFUL GIVER". I didn't always understand why the Lord was challenging me, but it was working for my good! How can you know God is a provider when you've NEVER been put in an uncomfortable position to know that He is one? Philippians 4:19 declares, "But MY GOD shall supply ALL your needs according to HIS riches in glory by Christ Jesus."

With a single-parent income, you MUST KNOW that it's the Lord, not the government! No one is happy to admit they're on welfare, but I'm on assignment to encourage some single mothers and remind them, this is NOT the end for you! You CAN build! A foundation starts from the ground up, but you MUST know what foundation is all about, WHAT it's built upon! IT MUST BEGIN WITH CHRIST! Build single mothers. Utilize what the Lord has put in YOUR hands. It won't happen overnight, but dig deep and build. Trust God! We are coming out of this together. I, too, am rebuilding.

The Lord used Prophet Cedric Stanton in 2019 to tell me, "Not to be worried or concerned about my status." He prophesied about my future husband and said so many other profound things. But my status was something I needed to hear. When you're someone who's been on welfare and trying to strive as a single parent, it can be concerning. It has caused me to think of how my future spouse would perceive me. Would he think I'm trying to be comfortable? Would he recognize my hard efforts in PUSHING forward as a single mother in the things of God? Would he be understanding of my situation?

You begin to notice how people treat you. They may think you're beneath them. They categorize you, put you in a box, size you up, and figure they already know your story. If they only knew the TREASURE that the Lord has placed on the inside of me (And you, Sis)! Single mothers, be encouraged in this area. Just like I have to encourage myself, your current status is NOT permanent! It's NOT your final destination!

My mother used to tell me, "It's only what YOU ALLOW!" The Lord has much more for us to grab ahold of, and trust me, your future lies in the hands of the Master! There's something I learned in this current season: I don't care what you see; what did HE SAY? In other words, don't look at what it looks like; what did the Lord tell you?

Let me put it in another way. With the naked eye, it looks really crazy right now. But with the spiritual eye, it was completed in the Spirit when the Lord declared it. It just hasn't become TANGIBLE yet in the natural world, but it will! Don't get discouraged! I know what it's like to have graduated high school, college background and working jobs that you don't enjoy. Still, you feel stagnated. You've pushed! My God! When will something BREAK or GIVE?

Single mothers, we've tried everything else; why not turn the will over to Jesus?! During this pandemic, the Lord has opened tremendous doors for me. I heard His voice and stepped out in faith. As a result, He is blessing the work of my hands! Don't let the struggle of welfare be your stopping point. It's time to push beyond this experience. Welfare may be a part of our struggle, but it won't be our final story! Jesus is the author and finisher of our faith. Let Him complete it!

CHAPTER 2:

The Impact On My Children

Children are a blessing and a gift from God! Their innocence is evident, and they don't ask to partake in the messes we create. I want to encourage some single ladies without children to consider the cost and be MINDFUL before having them. It's a blessing to plan and allow the Lord to show you HIS PLAN for your future family. Don't be eager, but take your time! As a young lady, I didn't get a chance to plan or think things through. I went straight into motherhood months after graduating high school, and I was NOT married. Know this: Who you become ONE with is going to shape many things for your future family. What MANY parents fail to realize is that the Lord has entrusted us with our children, and we are going to be held accountable as we are raising them!

Let's make one thing clear to single mothers. You can NEVER be both mom and dad. I don't care what people tell you! Have you ever received a comment from someone around Father's Day that because the other parent was absent, you're like both? They meant well, but they were wrong! Any of us that gladly accepted this comment, we too, were in error and should've been rebuked!

Though we've taken on MANY tasks as single mothers throughout the years, it doesn't mean we're permitted to take the credit for the father role. Here's why: The Bible declares in Ephesians 5:23, "For the husband is the HEAD of the wife, even as Christ is the head of the church: and he is the saviour of the body." God gave the husband/father a very strategic role that we cannot fulfill as the mother. As single mothers, we have to allow God to cover during the waiting period. Isaiah 54:5 declares, "For thy Maker is thine husband; the LORD of hosts is his name, and thy Redeemer the Holy One of Israel; The God of the whole earth shall he be called."

First, know that God ALONE gets all the glory because, without Him, you would've never made it this far. Second, a woman can never teach a boy to be a man. Yes, the Lord can give you wisdom and insight in this area. He can teach you HOW to nurture, train, and raise them. But one thing is for sure, you CAN'T teach that boy to be a man! Think about this scenario: Though a mother has always been present in her child's life, have you ever wondered why the child would SEEK OUT the father? They're curious and want to know WHERE their dad is located. Though he hasn't been present, they will still mention how they miss and love him. However, in some cases, I've also seen where the child can grow to resent their father because of his absence. Deep down, I believe love is still there, but emotions may be getting the best of the child during that time. I, too, have been there!

My children have been troopers throughout their experience! However, there have been topical questions, and they've been inquisitive as to what happened between their mom and dad. This is why we must realize the significance of the Lord's desire for us to be fruitful and multiply within the confines of marriage. Families were meant to be built around marriage, not outside of it! It's like the domino effect!

When you make a specific decision, you affect the loved ones around you. Our children are taking a hard blow on the other end, and it's hurting them deep down inside. I believe healing is essential and needs to take place in order for the child to bounce back. Depending on the situation, if not dealt with properly, I believe issues may arise in one's life, rooted in their misunderstandings and experiences in adolescence and adulthood. Facing the reality of the father not being there is key.

As a single Christian mother, had I known the hurt caused towards my children, I would've been more earnest with my planning. My pregnancies were unplanned, and I put my pleasure before the reality or outcome of my decision. Lord, I REPENT! How selfish can we be, not considering the agony we will cause our future seed? The problem is, we aren't cautious of another's future. Haggai 1:5 declares to us, "Now therefore thus saith the LORD of hosts; CONSIDER your ways." It's simple. We need to take MANY things into consideration.

Everyone's story isn't quite like mine. Perhaps you're a single mother who was raped or thought getting pregnant with a boyfriend might cause him to put a ring on it. Some of you may have been married to the father of your children, but things didn't go as planned, and you ended up in a devastating divorce. Whatever the situation, we've got to accept that there will be some effect on the child/children we're raising. The reactions will not be the same, but there's a solution to the problem!

Be encouraged! Jesus is the answer! Thank God for the prayers of the righteous, whether we are aware of them or NOT! The prayers are coverings. It all goes back to healing. Exodus 15:26, at the end of the passage, the LORD declared, "For I am the LORD that healeth thee." Glory To God! I know I've cried MANY tears as I've thought about the reactions and responses of my children during this process. I would often tell them how sorry I was for what they had to go through. With a simple response, they would reply with, "It's ok, mom." That soft-spoken response is enough to make you melt down in tears even more. It hurts! (The innocence is so pure.)

Together, with the help of the Lord, my children and I are daily working through the current situation we're in. Just us! God has been faithful and has taken care of us! Single mothers, understand that you CAN make it! It may have impacted our children, but WE ALL ARE SURVIVING!

CHAPTER 3:

What God Requires From You

There are MANY things that the Lord requires from us, but I will start by saying, He wants to be FIRST! Putting the Lord first is definitely a requirement. However, that's a decision you'll have to make. In Revelation 2:4, Jesus warned the church of Ephesus and declared, "Nevertheless I have somewhat against thee, because thou hast LEFT THY FIRST LOVE." During our season of singleness, it's IMPERATIVE that we make Jesus our FIRST LOVE. NEVER put something or someone in that spot! As I can attest that the LORD will remove the very thing you place above or before HIM.

Remember, God is a jealous God, and He's not taking second place to another. Exodus 34:14 declares, "For thou shalt worship no other god: for the LORD, whose NAME is Jealous, IS a jealous God:" In Deuteronomy 6:5-6, the Bible also declares, "And thou shalt love the LORD thy God with ALL thine heart, and with ALL thy soul, and with ALL thy might. And these words, which I command thee this day, shall be in thine HEART:" This is SO important, that we are reminded again in another passage of Scripture, where Jesus is talking to a lawyer in Matthew 22:37-38. Jesus said unto him, "Thou shalt LOVE the LORD thy God with ALL thy heart, and with ALL thy soul, and with ALL thy mind. This is the FIRST and GREAT COMMANDMENT." One verse of Scripture says, with all thy MIGHT, the other says with all thy MIND! That my dear is LOVING HIM with ALL OF YOU! (Something we ALL must strive for daily!)

Which brings me to point #2: I've learned that the Lord wants our ALL! He wants ALL of you, not some of you. Partiality just won't do! The Lord also wants a FULL YES from us! Total and complete surrender to

HIS WILL and NOT your own. Someone once asked the question, "Is He LORD over your life?" This doesn't JUST pertain to certain areas of your life, but all areas and in everything you do. That's a CHALLENGE!

In our singleness season, I'm learning the time is NOW to be very busy for God. Let your focus be on HOW YOU CAN PLEASE HIM! It's not always easy because our flesh has a way of making us feel as though we're alone. Those days often come for me, but the moment I'm reminded of marriage being like a ministry, I begin to thank God for my WAIT. When I hear about situations that married couples must ENDURE, I'm reminded of the APPOINTED TIME! (Wait for it!) This is a good spot to thank God for your SINGLENESS SEASON, though it has required MUCH patience. He's preparing us!

Pleasing HIM, point #3! The Scriptures are full of insight when it comes to those who are single. In 1 Corinthians 7:32-34, the Bible declares, "But I would have you without carefulness. He that is UNMARRIED careth for the things that belong to the Lord, HOW HE MAY PLEASE THE LORD: But he that is married careth for the things that are in the world, HOW HE MAY PLEASE HIS WIFE. There's also a difference between a wife and a virgin. The UNMARRIED woman careth for the things of the Lord that she may be HOLY both in body and in spirit: but she that is married careth for the things of the world, HOW SHE MAY PLEASE HER HUSBAND." Our main focus is how we may PLEASE the Lord! And no, it doesn't stop when hubby comes; it's continuous!

Something else the Lord requires from us is OUR TIME, point #4! Time spent allows us to develop INTIMACY with the Father, Son, and Holy Spirit, for they are ONE! The Bible declares in 1 John 5:7, "For there are THREE that bear record in heaven, the FATHER, the WORD, and the HOLY GHOST: and these THREE ARE ONE." When we make time to commune with the Lord, we then develop RELATIONSHIP. He gets to know us, and we get to know Him! Intimacy and relationship are important to develop while in your singleness with the Lord. In so much that when a husband comes, you are then not lost, scrambling to find your identity, but rather you already know WHO YOU ARE and YOUR ASSIGNMENT in the Body of Christ.

Our relationship and intimacy makes room for Him to make us the BEST we can be IN HIM. He's able to tell us about ourselves, like the areas that need to be developed, methods for our growth, and areas needing improvement! Many of us don't realize this type of communication with God is a requirement. The Lord has to shine HIS LIGHT on the areas in our life where we need DELIVERANCE. It's imperative so we don't contaminate that which God wants to release to us.

Point #5: Is a prayer life! A solid prayer life is a requirement as well. This too could attach itself to intimacy. Your prayer life, in its simplest form, is your communication with God. Dialogue! What SUSTAINS your relationship with Him? Without a prayer life, how will you be able to hear the voice of God and be led by Him? It's simple; you can't! If we position ourselves to HEAR Him while in prayer, you can NEVER go wrong! 1 Thessalonians 5:17 declares, "Pray without ceasing." Or how about Matthew 26:40, Jesus said, "Watch and pray, that ye enter NOT into temptation: the spirit indeed is willing, but the flesh is weak." If we are honest, our flesh gets very weak during our waiting because we're human. However, this does NOT give us the permission to give into it. The SPIRIT is willing, but the flesh will ALWAYS be weak! Stay willing!

Point #6: Obedience! The Lord has a way of taking you out of your comfort zone, and your obedience is required with it! I've realized during my walk with Jesus that obedience will take you to the next checkpoint. God can give instructions. But if you don't OBEY them, what use is it? Obedience comes with a great sacrifice, willingness, dedication, discipline, a made-up mind, and again, our SINCERE YES to the Lord. The Lord has a way of testing our obedience. The Bible tells us to obey is better than sacrifice (See 1 Samuel 15:22).

Finally, point #7: Your patience! The definition of patience can be defined as the CAPACITY to accept or tolerate delay, trouble, or suffering without getting angry or upset. Wow! Do we have what it takes to wait or remain calm when it seems as though NOTHING is going as planned? (I'm talking to myself here!) When you look at the definition of patience in the Hebrew language, it's defined as tolerance, moderation, temperance, mildness, and prudence. I'm being challenged here! Luke 29:19, Jesus declared, "In your patience possess ye your souls." I'm also reminded of the FRUIT of the Spirit that's to be produced and brought forth in the believer. Galatians 5:22-23 declares, "But the fruit of the Spirit is love, joy, peace, longsuffering, gentleness, goodness, faith, Meekness, temperance: against such, there is no law."

In our patience, can we understand that the Lord is at work? Can we see the MANY benefits that come with waiting? Can we see that while patience is being produced in us, it's working on our attitude and character? What's our outlook on our current situation as we remain patient? There's so much that's attached to our patience even in the building up of our faith! I was able to share these 7 points with you, because the Lord brought them to mind as I wrote. Currently, they're the very things He's bringing forth in me. I hope these 7 points have challenged areas within us as to what God requires from us!

CHAPTER 4:

Preparing Your Heart

In today's society, we are told to follow our hearts. That saying has been around for so long. But many of us know it's an error. It's a false statement! In so much that it contradicts what the Word of God tells us. Jeremiah 17:10 declares, "The heart is deceitful above ALL things, and desperately wicked: who can know it?" Your heart is capable of doing so much damage all by itself!

How many times have our hearts led us astray and misguided us? It was by the wickedness of our hearts that we got ourselves into toxic relationships, caused someone pain, and said things that affected someone's view of themselves. Some of us may say, "I didn't mean to say what I said to them." But I'm here to tell you that Jesus declared something very straightforward to the Pharisees. Matthew 12:34 says, "O generation of vipers, how can ye, being evil, speak good things? For out of the abundance of the HEART the mouth speaketh." What you verbalized during that time was EXACTLY what was lying dormant in your heart! The Lord had to do some reconstruction of our hearts! Because of all the wrong teachings we've learned from the world, we had to go back and relearn everything from our Father. David said it best in Psalm 51:2, 10-11, "WASH ME THOROUGHLY from mine iniquity, and cleanse me from my sin. Create in me a CLEAN HEART, O God, and RENEW a right spirit within me. Cast me not away from thy presence, and take not thy holy spirit from me."

The Lord knew we needed His precious Son Jesus to teach us HOW and WHAT to do! Why? Because we were born into sin. Within that same chapter, Psalm 51:5 declares, "Behold, I was shapen in iniquity; and in sin did my mother conceive me." Because of Adam's transgression, we are born into sin. Therefore we must be born again through Jesus Christ our Lord! Romans 5:12 and 14 declares, "Wherefore, as by ONE MAN sin entered into the world, and death by sin; and so death passed upon all men, for that ALL have sinned:" 14, "Nevertheless death reigned from Adam to Moses, even over them that had NOT sinned after the similitude of Adam's transgression, who is the figure of him that was to come."

I'm reminded of when Samuel went to anoint David as King. Samuel was being taught to NOT look at the way a man's OUTER appearance is, but rather look at HIS HEART. 1 Samuel 16:7 declares, "But the LORD said unto Samuel, Look NOT on his countenance, or on the height of his stature; because I have refused him: for the LORD seeth NOT as man seeth; for man looketh on the OUTWARD appearance, but the LORD looketh on the heart."

Have you ever had that moment where you've looked at a man and thought to yourself, "He's so handsome!" There's something about the way he carries himself. But the moment you hear what comes out of his mouth, you're in disgust? It's because the condition of this man's heart isn't in the right position. What you put on display IS what it is! Jesus declared in Matthew 15:11, "Not that which goeth INTO the mouth defileth a man; but that which cometh OUT of the mouth, THIS defileth a man." In other words, it's not so much about what you eat that defiles, but what comes out of your mouth can defile you! (By no means am I saying you shouldn't consider what you eat. We should be healthy as well. For better phrasing: be careful what you speak! This starts with being cautious as to what we're retaining in our heart, mind, and spirit! Be full of the WORD OF GOD and not of ourselves. Proverbs 23:7 also declares, "For as he thinketh in his HEART, so is he:" ...We should never think more highly of ourselves then we ought (See Romans 12:3).

There are times we're led to believe our heart is healed from previous experiences, when in fact, there's a process. We perceive the absence of the situation or the process of passing time has made us whole, but our perception is off. We are STILL broken in certain areas. How do we know this? Because when you REVISIT an event in your life, you're still BITTER or have some kind of emotion that manifests concerning it! There's a residue of the past, and the seeds that were planted, haven't yet been plucked up from the root. You MUST face-off and deal with it head-on! Take it to the Lord!

In my first book, "Single Mothers and Living For Christ," I hit on how "Healing is A Must." I can't stress that enough! When the Lord is preparing our hearts, He wants us to be made WHOLE IN HIM. Your healing plays a major role in preparing your heart for what God wants to do! This year, prophecies were still coming forth about the healing of MY heart. Even now, while I write, I'm appalled at the years of preparation, the purging, and deliverance that MUST take its place before proceeding! (Yikes) All because our hearts are STILL WOUNDED. Who would've thought historical events in our lives could be such a stronghold to your NEXT! However, I had to understand the Lord wants to prepare our hearts.

What we fail to understand is our hearts can STILL be entangled with those touchy subjects. Though with your mouth, you verbalized how it doesn't bother you. Have you TRULY healed? Did you TRULY turn it over to Jesus? Or after you laid it on the altar, did you pick it back up with your mind and emotions again? If this incident is still coming up repeatedly in every conversation you have and there are still emotions that have you in an uproar, perhaps it's time to re-evaluate if you've healed PROPERLY.

During this pandemic, I've had some time to reflect on my life. Where I'm at in the positioning of my heart. Where my relationship with Jesus is truly and where He's trying to take me. I've been sticking real close, and the closer I get to Him, the more He reveals my heart. I've learned no matter how minor a situation is concerning your heart, God wants to deal with it. He won't stop until you're FULLY CLEAN!

For the first time, I experienced self-deliverance! I remember the Lord telling me how I needed to prepare for my future spouse a few years ago. I didn't understand what He meant, and I was bold enough to ask Him, "Preparation how?" Within that same moment, He began to list all the things I needed healing from when it came to past relationships. I was shocked! (CHECKMATE!) I then began to follow His instructions in asking to be healed from these things. Sometimes we think we're ready for what we've been asking to be released, but it's not time!

The Lord knows the EXACT timing and when our heart is ready to accept what He's getting ready to do. I'd felt I was going to go through deliverance, and the Lord made me very aware of it.

On November 6th, 2020, I believe the Lord expressed these words to me:

Time for another level of purification...

It is being reached, daughter...

Come up...

The media has become a distraction for you...

But I am revamping you...

Every stronghold shall be loosed, and you shall be able to break free into another dimension in me...

Where you have been stuck, you shall no longer be stagnated...

But you shall burst forth...

Trust me with you, daughter...

Embrace me in a whole new way...

Even the pressures of your mind...

One thing that really stuck out to me in the prophetic message was REVAMP. Which means to renovate, rebuild, update, reconstruct, makeover, re-equip, upgrade, refurbish, remodel, redesign, recondition, improve and renew. My goodness! That word alone had me saying WOW! It was days after that a friend of mine by the name of Apostle WisePreach, confirmed the word of the Lord. It was revealed to him that the Lord was going to take me through deliverance from past relationships. I told him it was confirmation and that the Lord had revealed this to me very recently. I was a bit nervous because I didn't know what this kind of deliverance would entail. I'd never been here before. Sure, I had experienced where the Lord would purge me on different occasions, but there was something different about this deliverance that was getting ready to break forth.

One week, I'd been feeling queasy and was spitting up. I knew my purification was coming forth. I then went into another week where the queasiness returned with the spitting up, and still, I knew the Lord was doing what He said He would do. On Apostle WisePreach's YouTube live, I tuned in, and the Lord was already at work. The presence of the Lord was so strong, and the Glory of the Lord began to come forth. The Man of God began to tell us that people were getting ready to go through deliverance and that some of us would shake uncontrollably and some of us would vomit. Well, I happened to be one of the ones that vomited! The way the Lord laid His hand on me was ever so gently. Many of us know vomiting is not pleasant, but the way the Lord did it was graceful. I already had a sack prepared next to me in my room, and after releasing it, I felt so light.

The vomiting was not massive but unsubstantial. I was told that though it was minor, a massive deliverance took place. I was even told I sounded different! Glory To God! I was overjoyed that night and became excited! I began to think about how the Lord loves me enough to come to see about me. He came to deliver Tréasa Brown! Hallelujah!

When the Lord prepares your heart, He begins to expose it! Sometimes we tend to run from exposure because we don't want to see our TRUE SELF. But thank God for revealing that there IS such a thing as healthy exposure! It's to help identify the root of the issue. The saints of old used to say something along the lines of, "Lord, if you find anything that shouldn't be, take it out!" The Lord wants to prepare your heart! Perhaps there's residue in your heart that hasn't been dealt with by the Master. I encourage you, let Jesus deal with it so you can move on! Preparing your heart may not always be easy, but I've found out it's NECESSARY!

CHAPTER 5:

Did You Learn Your Lesson?

Life is full of lessons. Through every season of our lives, there's a different test. It's like going to school, taking a specific subject or grade, and discovering at the end of the semester if you pass or fail. If we don't pass a test or class, we retake it! Perhaps we really thought after taking a certain test, we did well. However, the test results showed otherwise! Have you ever felt like you were in a repeated cycle? Or felt like you're revisiting the SAME THING? That's because there's a lesson to be learned!

The Bible declares to us in Proverbs 4:7, "Wisdom is the principal thing; therefore get wisdom: and with ALL thy getting get UNDERSTANDING." If we don't have wisdom in a thing, we can always turn to the Lord and ask Him for it! James 1:5-8 declares, "If any of you LACK wisdom, let him ASK OF GOD, that giveth to all men liberally, and upbraideth not; and it shall be given him. But let him ask in FAITH, nothing wavering. For he that wavereth is like a wave of the sea driven with the wind and tossed. For let not that man think that he shall receive any thing of the Lord. A DOUBLE MINDED MAN is unstable in all his ways."

I've found myself in MANY cycles and have wondered why the same events keep occurring in my life. I didn't learn what God wanted me to learn! In fact, sometimes, I would choose the same thing, thinking it would produce a different outcome. (WRONG! INSANITY!) I needed maturity and growth! (Still at it!) I had to CHOOSE DIFFERENTLY!

Choosing the same thing will NOT get you different results. Why do we think that sometimes? You'll remain stagnant, unproductive, and infertile. Choose again! Hear me. Years can pass you by, you can age gracefully and STILL not learn your lesson! It's time to be optimistic. Pass the test and learn from it!

As mentioned in chapter 1, I'm learning repetitive cycles MUST be broken in the spirit! Sure, you can CHOOSE some things to stop doing on your own, but others MUST be uprooted in the spirit! The Bible declares to us in 1 Corinthians 15:46, "Howbeit that was not first which is spiritual, but that which is NATURAL; and AFTERWARD that which is spiritual." In other words, do what is natural first, THEN spiritual.

Everyone has a level of experience. No matter what it was, it should've taught us something. You do live and learn, experience is really a good teacher. But NO ONE can teach us like the Holy Ghost! He's the BEST teacher! John 14:26, Jesus declares, "But the Comforter, which is the Holy Ghost, whom the Father will send in my name, he shall TEACH you all things, and bring ALL THINGS to your remembrance, whatsoever I have said unto you."

Single ladies, when it comes to life experiences, there are routes you DON'T have to choose. However, taking notes, listening, and observing helps as a lesson all by itself. You don't have to pick it or live it, but rather avoid it! Let the spirit of God lead you into ALL truth! You might be led astray by your OWN feelings, but HE will NEVER lead you astray!

As a single mother, I've learned about the consequences of life. The decisions you make matter and affect more than just you! My children were affected to a certain capacity by some of the choices I made. We are still facing some of them today. However, the Lord is merciful and is bringing us through it! We rarely think about the long-term effects when caught up in the MOMENT. I've learned to THINK before I act on it. Particular situations had me caught up in my emotions rather than reflecting on the Word of God. You'd be surprised how much further you'll come along when your emotions are REMOVED from the equation.

I'm discovering we quote Scripture, preach, teach, and prophesy, but HOW will we really begin to APPLY the Word of God to our life? After one has studied for a test, one must apply. What are we learning as we're applying these things? (Lesson: APPLICATION matters!) We don't have to pick a replica, and it's ok to say NO! Keep your future and that which God has for YOU and destiny in the forefront! With specific lessons, there's no do-over, and you'll be working with what you've got. But as you work with it, REFLECT!

I've learned that distractions WILL come, but don't be deterred by them! Keep moving! These hindrances come to slow you down! Proverbs 4:25-27 declares, "Let thine eyes look right on, and let thine eyelids look straight before thee. PONDER the path of thy feet, and let all thy ways be established. Turn not to the right hand nor to the left: remove thy foot from evil."

What I gathered from this Scripture is not to look at what's happening on every side of you. Look forward! Think about where you're going in life. Keep things set in place and abstain from wrongdoing! The tests we go through may not always be what we're expecting. Have you ever taken an exam that you know you studied for, and seemingly none of what you reviewed was on the test? This happens! For incidences we come across in life that we didn't sign up for, this is where our faith has to be stretched. No, it's NOT EASY! Even though it's not our preference, we must trust God!

I've learned the enemy doesn't play fair. If you don't learn and apply wisdom, he will keep you ignorant. 2 Corinthians 2:11 declares, "Lest Satan should get an advantage of us: for we are NOT ignorant of HIS DEVICES." He comes on assignment to steal, kill and destroy (John 10:10). The Bible also tells us in 1 Peter 5:8, "Be sober, be vigilant; because your adversary the devil, as a roaring lion, walketh about, SEEKING whom he may devour."

Single mothers, when life throws us a curveball, Jesus is the one we can always turn to, to help us swing the bat! Much has been thrown my way, but I learned how to humble myself under the MIGHTY hand of God. It taught me to pray! The Clark Sisters sang it best, "Though we are tried, like silver in the fire, we come out as pure gold. We must be refined, and then we need a shine; we come out as pure gold...."

We must be tried and tested as a maidservant of God! Have I been tried on the same level as others? Absolutely not! But there will come a time where we will all be tested on another level! 1 Peter 4:12-13 declares, Beloved, think it not strange concerning the fiery trial which is to try you as if some strange thing happened unto you: But rejoice, insomuch as ye are partakers of Christ's sufferings; that when his glory shall be revealed, ye may be glad also with exceeding joy." Situations can seem very odd at the moment, to the point where we wonder, "Is this really happening to me?"

Consider these MINOR tests that we endure in life as practice, because there's a GREATER TRIAL coming to every believer! That's a totally different subject, which I've not yet reached! The Lord will NOT test us at a grade level if we are unprepared. You'll be tested right where you are, at grade level, in the spirit. However, some of us might test up and out, according to the wisdom God gave us! Exceeding our very own expectations because we APPLIED the help of the Father!

There's a specific thing my mother would say to me that captured my attention. She would say, "The test is about YOU." I now understand what she meant! Often when we've had a fallout with a person, whether it was a relationship, friendship, or marriage, something was to be grasped. We're known to blame, point the finger, and say, "It's their fault." But what if I told you it's an opportunity TO GROW? I'm not saying be a rug or doormat for someone to walk over. But did it ever occur to you to be quiet?

What we fail to realize is observing OURSELVES in the matter is essential to our growth. Our CHARACTER is not only being DEVELOPED but TESTED! Do we always have to have a response for EVERYTHING? You know, there's STRENGTH in being quiet! In Isaiah 30:15, the second portion of that stanza declares, "In quietness and in confidence shall be your strength." ... 1 Thessalonians 4:11 declares, "And that ye study to be quiet, and to work with your own hands, as we commanded you; " 1 Peter 3:4 also declares, "But let it be the hidden man of the heart, in that which is not corruptible, even the ornament of a MEEK and QUIET SPIRIT, which is in the sight of God of GREAT PRICE."

Whatever test you face, remember you've got aid to assist you! What have you learned?

CHAPTER 6:

Spiritual Growth

We often focus on our physical man (FLESH). Our shape, size, height, physical attributes, if you will. Adorning ourselves with makeup, jewelry, perfume, and the best apparel. We get physically fit and consider our nutritional diet. Nothing wrong with these things. However, what's wrong is neglecting the Spirit man!

I'm reminded of a fair and beautiful woman in the Bible by the name of Esther (See Esther 2:7). She "obtained favour in the sight of all them that LOOKED upon her." (Esther 2:14) The King loved her above all the women, and she obtained grace and favor in the sight of the king, more than all the virgins (Esther 2:17). You see, Esther couldn't come before the King in any kind of way. There was protocol! Esther 2:12 declares, "Now when every maid's turn was come to go in to king Ahasuerus, after that she had been TWELVE MONTHS, according to the manner of the women, (for so were the days of their purifications accomplished, to wit, SIX MONTHS with oil of myrrh, and SIX MONTHS with sweet odours, and with other things for the purifying of the women)."

Though there was physical preparation, there was much more required! Esther was not just fair and beautiful, but she applied WISDOM when Haman sought to kill the Jews. She proclaimed a 3 day fast and went before the King unsummoned. Doing this could've cost her life! What's your point, woman of God? Esther wasn't just posted up looking cute. She had to KNOW her God! She had a position, an assignment in the King's palace, and it was beyond her beauty!

How do we look in the Spirit? Do we know WHO we are in the Spirit? What would the Lord show us beyond our natural self? We're talking about the REAL YOU! In my first book, "Single Mothers and Living for Christ," I briefly hit on how we are made in God's image and likeness, according to Genesis 1:27. I spoke on "your Spirit Man is the real authentic you!" In the last chapter, we briefly hit on the first natural, then spiritual. Yes indeed! However, our Spirit Man is ignored. Just like we nurture the physical body, nurture the Spirit!

Single mothers, if we're spending all this time perfecting our looks, why not our Spirit Man? Let me interject here for a moment. A REAL MAN will want more than JUST a woman's physical appearance and far more than JUST her body. If that's the case, sorry ladies, as my brother Tony Brown likes to say: "He's not ready for prime time!" Rather, he'll want to know your MIND! How about a woman who is educated and will encourage his vision!? A woman who fears the Lord! Psalm 31:30 declares, "Favor is deceitful, and beauty is vain: but a woman who feareth the LORD, she shall be praised." Someone who can undergird, cover and help birth the ministry God gave him, support, challenge and affirm him! One who knows her identity in God and has access to the Father (A prayer life)! I'm referring to those who have a REAL relationship with God. An authentic anointing! This, my dear, comes with spiritual growth! But we WON'T discern a real man if we keep going by the standards of the world.

The Spirit Man needs to be fed with the Word of God! Like a newborn baby, he/she will not grow and function properly because of malnourishment. There will be severe and detrimental issues within the brain that can cause stagnation. They can become dysfunctional and development can lag. It is the same with the Spirit.

When you're NOT fed with the Word of God, contamination is bound to occur. You're easily swayed, tricked, and confused because you've not READ the Scriptures pertaining to your life. There becomes a void in your life, an emptiness, a longing that your Spirit Man needs. The Spirit recognizes it's a NECESSITY, but your flesh causes you to neglect it! This can cause uncertainty in one's life and at the end, spiritual death! One needs to commune with Father, Son, and Holy Ghost. John 14:23, "Jesus answered and said unto him, If a man loves me, he will keep my words: and my Father will love him, and we will come unto him, and make OUR ABODE with him."

What MANY don't realize is, you can be a walking dead man. How so? One can be very much alive in the physical body. But because you've not chosen Christ as your Saviour and are NOT FILLED WITH HIS SPIRIT, you're still connected to a dying world! Romans 8:8-9 declares, "So then they that are in the flesh cannot please God. But ye are not in the flesh, but in the Spirit, if so be that the Spirit of God DWELL IN YOU. Now if any man have NOT the Spirit of Christ, he is NONE of his." That Scripture is weighty! In addition, Colossians 3:1-3 declares, "If ye then be risen WITH CHRIST, seek those things which are above, where Christ sitteth on the right hand of God. Set your affection on the things ABOVE, not on things on the EARTH. For ye are DEAD, and your life is HID with Christ IN God."

You see, to be RISEN with Christ, is to DIE TO YOURSELF. What do you mean? Your sinful ways, your sinister lifestyle, your ways to this world MUST go! Say goodbye! This is a daily process, a challenge! This takes the help of the Lord to TAME your flesh! You will always be in a fleshly body as long as you live on this earth. This is why we NEED the Spirit of God (But die DAILY to your flesh)! Galatians 5:16 declares, "This

I say then, Walk in the Spirit, and ye will NOT fulfil the lust of the FLESH."

If we are walking after the Spirit, then that means it's something we're pursuing after! The flesh CAN'T bring you to where the Spirit can. It's in the Spirit, where you will catch revelations that the flesh can't reveal. When walking in the Spirit, you're able to SEE beyond what the naked eye can't. This is why we need spiritual growth, and maturity in another dimension. For example, ladies, when you're viewing things with the natural eye, it's not enough! At times, to grasp the fullness of a situation, the Lord opens your spiritual eyes, and you begin to see FURTHER.

Those who GROW in the Spirit and SEE spiritual things have such an advantage! This is why we must continue to pursue the things of God. That we may MATURE and become the woman God is calling us to be IN HIM. There will come a time where our beauty will fade... Let's flourish and grow in grace, but in the Spirit. Expand with me!

CHAPTER 7:

The Lord Will Keep You Hidden

Hidden is defined as kept out of sight, concealed, veiled, and unrevealed. In the Greek, it means to cover, conceal, keep secret. Pronounced krymménos (Secret, undercover, mystical, clandestine and privy). During my time of walking with Jesus and communing with Him, I discovered He had me hidden in MANY different seasons of my walk. For example, when I first started discovering who I was in Him and the prophetic call on my life, God had me in the wilderness season.

What do I mean? A season where it's just you and God. No friends around, and it seems like everybody has been cut off. You're in isolation, in a good way, though you feel you're alone. When wilderness comes to mind, we think of dry places, nothing around for miles, a place where you're unproductive, a drought, and nothing grows.

I beg to differ. I've learned you can be VERY productive during this season! I had to look at this season from another perspective. With Jesus, you'll be alright! The Bible declares in Isaiah 43:19, "Behold, I will do a NEW thing; now it shall spring forth; shall ye not know it? I will even make a way in the wilderness, and rivers in the desert."

When you're going through a wilderness season, a NEW THING is sure to come forth in the end. The Lord will provide! That's your time to draw near to Him, hear Him, and keep everyone else out of your ears. A time to block bad influences, discern and reflect. There, I was TRAINED to hear His voice (while journaling). I discovered my identity, cultivated intimacy, and I began to grow in Him. These seasons come and go and you'll have MORE than one. (Especially as a prophet or prophetic voice). It's imperative!

In the past, over time, I discovered something interesting. At first, I was being approached by a lot of unsaved men. However, when I reached a certain season in my walk with God, I was no longer approached; neither did I attract the same flock of men. In fact, no one reached out for years. I was glad that I identified this change.

During that particular season, I ran across a woman of God (WOG) on YouTube, by the name of Prophetess Danielle Jean, who was speaking on "The Seed." To my surprise, she shared a specific example that resonated with my spirit. She expounded on the subject of being REAL good and saved, and no one is trying to "Holla" at you! (Smile) The God in her was saying, "It is the GLORY of the Lord resting on you!" But hold it, TESTS will come back around in different seasons. It goes back to being tried!

Single mothers, have you ever felt like the ONLY odd one out? That seemingly strange situation you're going through is JUST you? That was me here. I was so glad this WOG elaborated on that particular scenario. It wasn't by chance or coincidence I heard this message. I'm glad the Lord caused me to UNDERSTAND.

My friend, Prophetess Teneen Gainey, told me this year how the Lord showed her a vision of me slowly being unveiled. Prophet Cedric Wright II prophesied about no more hiding among the shadows and that God has given me permission. The list goes on...Why am I sharing this? The Lord will do everything in HIS timing because He knows when it's your season to come forth! We're talking about being hidden, remember. Like the baby that's hidden in the mother's womb, and after 9 months or less, the water breaks, and IT'S TIME for that baby to come forth out of the birth canal! There's no denying a baby has just been born.

Micah 4:10a declares, "Be in pain, and labour to bring forth, O daughter of Zion, like a woman in travail:" I must admit, though I mentioned isolation in a good way (and it is), it's not all fun and games. It hurts! You must push through feeling alone and embrace the unconditional love of God, knowing it's MORE THAN ENOUGH. It's timely because I've entered into another season of being alone even as I'm writing! During the beginning of January, I told myself, "I'm getting ready to walk alone." I felt it! The Lord allowed me to prophesy to myself. I'm grateful the LORD is helping me to discern the times, just like the sons of Issachar (See 1 Chronicles 12:32). In fact, it was prophesied over me! It's happening!

During the hidden season, I realize it's God's way of shielding you. Not just that, but He's cultivating you for what lies ahead. Like the clay on the potter's wheel, you MUST be made! Isaiah 64:8 declares, "But now, O LORD, thou art our father; WE ARE the clay, and THOU our potter; and we ALL are the work of thy hand." When on the potter's wheel, be prepared for things to SHIFT!

Sometimes being exposed too soon can abort the process and cause other complications to come. Whenever taken back to the wilderness, you can be sure you'll learn something there. Your season has changed! A WOG by the name of Pastor Leech called me out in a service and told me, "There's a difference between being hidden and overlooked..." She explained that I was hidden...Ladies, sometimes we get frustrated when we feel we're overlooked. But perhaps, like me, we misunderstand WHY we're hidden and forget it's for a PURPOSE! Perhaps like me, you're not overlooked!

You will not be revealed before your time! Treasures are HIDDEN! I've been told there's a treasure on the inside of me more than once. Something profound I discovered in high school is that my name means treasure! If you look at the EXACT spelling of my name, you'll see the first 5 letters of my name are T R E A S. All that's missing is the letter A, to make TREASA! I'm valuable in the sight of God, and so are YOU single mothers!

Sure, at times, we can feel like, "Does anybody see or hear me?" But you are seen and heard more than you think! Embrace being hidden before future relationships, ministry, while on the job, or whatever it is. God certainly knows what He's doing! It's only a matter of time before His treasures will no longer be hidden but found! Are you ready?

CHAPTER 8:

"He's Not Your Husband!"

One of the hardest lessons I've learned as a young lady was to OBEY the voice of God when I KNEW I heard Him and ignored it. It's one thing to hear Him, and it's another to obey! When He shows you...my God! You get a GOOD understanding of what He meant. Single mothers, we're so hard-headed at times (me), and we cause our pitfalls because we didn't heed the voice of God. We didn't pay CLOSE attention to the conviction we felt or the big red flags right in front of our faces! Why must we ignore these things!? The consequences are too severe when unnecessary routes are taken.

I believe it was around 2013 and I was about 24 years old when a major incident happened in my life. I was sharing testimonies on my YouTube channel and pursuing after the things of God. A young man ran across my page and sent compliments through comments on my videos. Before I knew it, the public comments became private inboxes. I saw a video of his, which led me to believe he was a believer. He talked about the things of God and portrayed himself as a Christian man. I rolled with it, but wasn't very discerning.

Soon the inboxes turned into extending my personal contact information. From there, we talked. He seemed sweet and charming, but at times the conversations would shift and get out of hand. He would talk about having sex. I knew our conversations were out of order, but when flesh rises, you get lured in. Note: MAJOR red flag! Any man that's talking about taking you to the bed is already leading you AWAY from the Lord, NOT to Him! He got serious, and he wanted to travel to Colorado.

Keep in mind, I'm a single mother of three beautiful children. What was I thinking? (Really) Ladies, it's NOT WISE to let a man you don't know come to your place of residence and bring him to your family too early. That comes with TIME! This is very dangerous! Not just for you, but your precious ones! Once again, Proverbs 4:7 declares, "WISDOM IS the principal thing; therefore GET wisdom: and with ALL thy getting get understanding." Proverbs 3:7, "Be not wise in thine OWN eyes; fear the LORD, and DEPART from evil."

Why did I entertain it? Desperation! I talked about this in my first book, "Single Mothers and Living for Christ." While it may sound like the man is serious, it can lead to disaster. Before he took a flight to Colorado, the Lord began to speak to me. I heard a voice say, "He's not your husband!" (I heard it very strongly) I dismissed the voice and avoided what I heard. I was trying to make a puzzle piece fit that didn't belong.

I remember praying about it, even though I KNEW what I heard. I HAD MY ANSWER! Specifically, I prayed about his flight, and it worked out. It really WAS coming all together after all! I received a second word. "He's not your husband, and I'm going to show you why."

I believe I heard this AFTER he came into town; it was loud and clear! Arriving in Colorado, my mother and I picked him up, and I drove him to my place. Note 2: It's deranged to go on the enemy's territory and bring him right into your house. By no means am I saying I was innocent in the matter. I was WRONG, and I should've listened to my Heavenly Father! As a single mother and living for Christ, Lord knows I knew better, and to know better means to DO BETTER!

Note 3: Cohabitation is becoming very common in our society today. The word itself was fairly new to me, but as I think about the concept, it's not so new, and people have been doing it for years. While studying a plan on my You Version Bible app, I came across this word for relationships and dating. Cohabitation is defined as the state of living together and having a sexual relationship without being married. Shockingly, this is happening in the Body of Christ. Standards are plummeting! Marriage benefits are now easy to attain without the consent of the Father. Dangerous! I'm glad I was not sexually involved with this young man and giving him benefits of what rightfully belongs to my future husband.

It wasn't long before the Holy Spirit began to deal with me more. It was heavy, like a weight! I started feeling conviction and warfare. It was to the point of crying and having deep regrets. God is such a good Father that way! Hebrews 12:6-8 declares, "For whom the LORD loveth he chasteneth, and scourgeth EVERY SON whom he receiveth. If ye endure chastening, God dealeth with you as with sons; for what son is he whom the father chasteneth not? But IF ye be without chastisement, whereof all are partakers, then are ye bastards, and NOT sons." Though in ERROR, I was STILL His daughter!

My Spirit Man was NOT in agreement with the flesh. They're CONTRARY to one another! Galatians 5:17 declares, "For the flesh lusteth against the Spirit, and the Spirit against the flesh: and these are contrary the one to the other: so that ye cannot do the things ye would." No wonder I felt so uneasy with NO PEACE! I knew I was in trouble. I cried out to God in my home. In my heavenly language to God, praying in tongues as this young man was rubbing on my back. My heart was sincere, but my actions didn't come in alignment.

It wasn't long before the revealing began. It was surfacing! There was literally a SHIFT! I received crazy text messages from him on my sister's cell phone, and it wasn't long before she noticed them. My younger sister discerned other red flags, long before she witnessed the text messages. (The Lord showed me alright!) I put my family in danger to the point of my big brothers escorting this young man out of my mother's home. I was ashamed! The lessons I've learned!...

I don't know about you, but if God can tell me who's NOT my husband, then certainly HE CAN reveal who is! This topic is very controversial, but I won't put God in a box. We say He's a BIG GOD, and He can do ANYTHING. However, we limit Him! Only letting Him operate in specific areas of our lives. Please STOP putting limits on God!

Let's explore for a moment. In Genesis 24, you'll discover that Abraham is talking to his eldest servant and gives him specific instructions concerning his son Isaac and finding his future wife. Whom we know to be Rebekah! He tells him SPECIFICALLY not to take a wife of the Canaanites (See Genesis 24:3). However, he tells him to go to his country, where his kindred is, and take a wife for his son. What captures my interest is, Abraham's servant is uncertain that the woman will follow him back to the land. As he makes his adventure, he prays to the Lord that the damsel will do specific things, so that he would KNOW God had APPOINTED this woman for Isaac.

Let's take a closer look. Genesis 24:12-14 declares, "And he said, O LORD God of my master Abraham, I pray thee, send me good speed this day and shew kindness unto my master Abraham. Behold, I stand here by the well of water; and the daughters of men of the city come out to draw water: And let it come to pass, that the damsel to whom I shall say, Let down thy pitcher, I pray thee, that I may drink; and she shall say, Drink, and I will give thy camels drink also: LET THE SAME BE SHE THAT THOU HAST APPOINTED FOR THY SERVANT ISSAC; and thereby shall I KNOW that thou hast shewed kindness unto my master."

Now take a look at the specification. Verse 18- 21, "And she said, Drink, my lord: and she hasted, and let down her pitcher upon her hand, and gave him drink. And when she had done giving him drink, she said, I will draw water for thy camels also, until they have done drinking. And she hasted, and emptied her pitcher into the trough, and ran again unto the well to draw water, and drew for ALL his camels. And the man WONDERING at her held his peace, to wit whether the LORD had made his journey prosperous or not." Verse 26-27, "And the man bowed down his head and worshiped the LORD. And he said, "Blessed be the LORD God of my master Abraham, who hath not left destitute my master of his mercy and his truth: I being in the way, the LORD LED ME to the house of my master's brethren."

I hope you ladies captured all that! God is an AWESOME GOD! When we acknowledge Him and ask Him specifics, can He not answer and show us? There's something about acknowledging the Lord, like the Word of God commands us, in ALL YOUR WAYS! The Scripture says, "and HE SHALL direct your paths" (See Proverbs 3:5-6). Why are you saying all this woman of God? Because I want the single mothers and single women, in general, to know there's hope for us!

No matter what your current situation has been, or currently is, the Lord will give inevitable direction and instruction. It's our positioning that needs alignment! The Lord can't release me to just anybody! I will discuss this in another chapter to come. The Lord has MANY ways of protecting us from things we can't see up ahead. When you see the caution tape ahead, don't get any closer! Don't proceed! STOP and turn around! We often continue, wanting to know the outcome. Our curiosity can come with a fine price tag! When you find out he's not the one, he's just not!

CHAPTER 9:

Are You Willing To Try Again?

Situations we've been through in life can really take a toll on us. We're weary in specific areas and want to give up. The repetitious cycles, disappointment after disappointment, the hurt, pain, and despair are overwhelming. What amazes me is how God created us to be more than conquerors despite these challenges! Romans 8:37 declares, "Nay, in all these things we are MORE than conquerors through HIM that loved us." No matter how detrimental, difficult, or heartbreaking a life situation was, the Lord still allowed us to get back up and keep pursuing.

Again is defined as, another time, once more or returning to a previous condition or position. Single mothers, perhaps the thought of getting into a relationship makes you cringe because of devastating heartbreak. Or going after that business you always dreamed of didn't work out, and you say, "Never again." Perhaps your first marriage failed because of infidelity, and you experienced an ugly divorce. Are you willing to try again? As humans we have failed repeatedly, but the sooner we realize Jesus NEVER fails, we may be willing to try it again. Only this time, WITH Jesus! You say, "That's cliche," but it's a fact! He will never fail us!

Just because you're saved and filled with the Holy Ghost doesn't mean you've always done it HIS WAY! Look at the testimonies I've shared. I was pursuing after God, but I didn't ALWAYS do everything HIS way necessarily. I failed in certain areas where I needed growth, but I tried again! Had I stayed in my condition, I wouldn't have conquered it without the help of the Lord. To conquer means to overcome and take control of successfully. A conqueror is one who wins; they're a victor, a champion! There's still much to conquer with Jesus on this journey. I'm grateful we'll always have the victory in HIM!

There are so many thoughts in my mind as a single mother when it comes to my future spouse. I know the Lord has spoken over my life concerning it, which ought to settle the restlessness in my mind. However, relationships have taken their cycle in my life, where it's taken a wrong turn EVERY TIME, and my heart is left broken. Being vulnerable is the issue here! You should always keep discernment in place and guard your heart. The Bible declares in Proverbs 4:23, "Keep your heart with all diligence; for out of it are the issues of life." When the Lord makes my heart WHOLE again in Him, will I be willing to try again? The answer is yes!

When you do it the Lord's way, you WILL have great success! Isaiah 55:8-9 declares, "For my thoughts are NOT your thoughts, neither are your ways my ways, saith the LORD. For as the heavens are higher than the earth, so are my ways higher than your ways, and my thoughts than your thoughts." During the moment of heartbreak, it feels unbearable. Like you can't bear it another time. (I love very hard) But thank God for restoration!

A particular woman of God brought something to my attention recently. The love God gave me is truly a gift! She was right! Everyone doesn't have it! We know that GOD IS LOVE (1 John 4:8)!

James 1:17 declares, "Every good gift and every perfect gift is from above, and cometh down from the Father of lights, with whom is no variableness, neither shadow of turning." For as long as I can remember, no matter what a man might've done to me in past relationships, I've always had this soft heart towards them while dating. Sure, different emotions took place during a time of hurt. If I received less than what I deserved, I still wanted to give 100% in the relationship. Are you able to give love AGAIN, knowing there's a risk of no reciprocation?

When I finally open up my heart and give love, why has it ALWAYS ended with heartbreak and rejection? Why Lord? Single mothers, you may feel you'll never get over a particular struggle. But you will! The unconditional love that God gives us is meant to be distributed, not held onto, even if there's NOTHING in return! That sounds harsh, but it's something to consider.

What have I learned in trying again, single mothers? Go for it once more, having LEARNED from previous mistakes. AVOID repeats that didn't work before and stick to your NO! It's ok to take a moment to reflect on WHY something didn't work out the first time. However, while you reflect, don't OVER ANALYZE IT. (That's me)

Look at your failures as a STEPPING STONE and a way to allow Jesus in! Don't be so quick to make a decision without asking your Heavenly Father FIRST. Present it before Him in prayer, WAIT, then ACT as instructions are given. Own up to what YOU DID, once acknowledged, confess and move on! Ask the Lord to restore and resuscitate you! The battle is not over! Try, Try again!

CHAPTER 10:

Not Just Anybody!

Anybody can be defined as any person or anyone. Out of all the relationships I've been in, I've come to understand the Lord WON'T let (Tréasa Brown) His daughter settle for JUST anybody. Why have ALL the relationships I've been in equaled a "No!?" Perhaps the Lord has a very strategic plan for me. It takes me back to my first book when the Lord spoke of: "The very best." You see, the definition of best is the most excellent, effective, or desirable type or quality (Supreme, finest, most excellent, matchless, ultimate, optimal or optimum). With God's hand in it, this can be attained.

It does NOT mean your future spouse will be flawless. We understand that no human is perfect, but Christ our Lord! It's possible to have the TRUE Man of God (MOG) for my children and I. I was told in a prophecy, the Lord is fully developing and maturing my husband and I, whoever he may be. As sanctified saints, we are BEING perfected. Transformation doesn't come overnight, but rather through a process! Hebrews 10:14 declares, "For by ONE offering he hath PERFECTED for ever them that are SANCTIFIED."

That one offering is Jesus, and we are supposed to allow Him to work on us DAILY! Growing and learning in our faith, laying aside every weight and sin that so easily besets us (See Hebrews 12:1). It takes patience! We are called to be perfect as our Father in Heaven. Matthew 5:48 declares, "Be ye PERFECT, even as your Father which is in heaven is perfect." In Hebrew, perfect means whole, complete, accomplished, and intact. Being whole and complete is found in Jesus!

Anybody can have somebody! So what IS God's very best, and just HOW will He do it for me? How will I know my hubby is "the one?" There are so many questions that reside in my mind. However, I'll need to trust God and take Him at His word.

Single mothers, the sooner you realize it's not God's will for you to be just anyone's "hook up," the better you understand this special someone must be linked up with your destiny and purpose! If not, it's to be discontinued! When you understand your purpose in God, your destiny begins to unfold and make sense. Certain things the Father may ask of us may not always register with our finite mind. For those of us that are currently STILL single, well, why are we? I believe our assignment is different, and there's a reason for it!

Imagine having a choice of so many different flavors of candy in a basket, but specific ones in particular, stand out. Which one has the potential to satisfy your taste buds? Perhaps it's the smell or the look of the candy. If someone only allowed you to choose JUST ONE out of the basket, I'm sure you'll think twice before making your selection.

I'm reminded of a man named Gideon in the book of Judges, where the Lord had specifically selected 300 men out of the 10,000 to go against the Midianites.

Judges 7:2-7 declares, "And the LORD said unto Gideon, The people that are with thee are TOO MANY for me to give the Midianites into their hands, lest Israel vaunt themselves against me, saying, Mine own hand hath saved me. Now, therefore, go to, proclaim in the ears of the people, saying, Whosoever is FEARFUL and AFRAID, let him return and depart early from mount Gilead. And there returned of the people twenty and two thousand; and there REMAINED ten thousand; And the LORD said unto Gideon, The people are yet TOO MANY; bring them down unto the water, and I will TRY THEM for thee there: and it shall be, that of whom I say unto thee, This shall go with thee, the same SHALL GO with thee; and of whomsoever I say unto thee, This shall not go with thee, the same shall NOT go. So he brought down the people unto the water: and the LORD said unto Gideon, Every one that lappeth of the water with his tongue, as a dog lappeth, him shalt thou set by himself; likewise, everyone that boweth down upon his knees to drink. And the number of them that lapped, putting their hand to their mouth, were three hundred men: but all the rest of the people bowed down upon their knees to drink water. And the LORD said unto Gideon, By the THREE HUNDRED men that lapped will I save you, and deliver the Midianites into thine hand: and let all the other people go every man unto his place."

How unique! Like the 300 men that lapped up the water in their hand, I believe there are some distinct and exclusive women of God reading this book, that you too, can't have JUST anyone! What's your point, Woman of God? Do you really believe you're set apart for your health? Or do you believe it's tied to purpose?

God is yet a specific God! The 300 that lapped up the water with their tongue were CHOSEN by God to deliver the Midianites into the hands of Gideon. The Lord has specific assignments for certain people that ARE chosen for a particular purpose for His Kingdom. Single mothers, consider it no minor thing when the Lord SPECIFIES the steps He wants you to take with Him in life. Even when it comes to a "destiny helper!" Some people are NOT assigned to you, and they will not partake in your destiny. They may have STARTED with you, but they will not FINISH with you! This is a hard truth, but it's facts!

Am I complicating relationships in my life? Or does it have to do with my anointing and purpose? Have I missed God by not taking what's been offered before me? For me, it has seemed there's been a hold-up on marriage in my life. However, the wait I truly believe has been for the best. I don't always understand what the Lord is doing, but as I walk with Him, I've had to trust that HE KNOWS what He's doing!

Have you ever prayed replicated prayers for years, and sometimes there's no answer from the Lord right then? Or, an answer soon comes, but it's just enough to keep you in a place of faith and trust? THE WAITING PERIOD! Waiting on Him is the ONLY option, and it can't be rushed or hurried! However, people do have FREE WILL and POWER OF CHOICE.

Many times, the Lord is waiting on us! Alignment with HIS WILL and NOT our own. I don't know about you ladies, but there's something about the wait that's very complicated. You know there's a purpose for it, but it's challenging over time! Some of you reading this book may say, "It's simple to get married; just let it happen, and give someone a chance." If you really understood the "weight" of certain men and women of God's anointing, you would understand it's not that simple. (Remember chapter 8, He's NOT Your Husband?)

People have jumped ahead of God and didn't wait. They were married outside of the WILL of God! As a result, their marriage became a tragedy, a disaster! Wait is defined as the ability to stay where one is or delay action until a PARTICULAR time. Or until something happens! (Wait, await, hold on or hang on) It sounds less appealing. But when you look at the Hebrew definition of waiting, it means to hope, expect or look forward to. There's more of a climax!

As we know, a climax is the MOST exciting or important part of the story. From the beginning until then, there can be so much between victories, failures, sunshine, rain, breakthroughs, and setbacks. But when reaching the top of THAT mountain, it feels tremendous knowing it was worth the climb all along! Though you couldn't see what was ahead, your journey wasn't in vain!

Most importantly, Jesus was there all the time! When you didn't feel equipped enough to speak to the mountain, you spoke to it anyway, and the Lord moved on your behalf; you overcame with HIS HELP! When you thought you were going to fall off a cliff. Meaning, you came to an end point and felt like giving up. He held you by your right hand and kept you! When you didn't have the endurance to take another step on your own, Jesus was your strength and carried you through it! What more can our mighty God do!?

With that in mind, let's take a look at Scripture. In Mark 11:23, Jesus declares, "For verily I say unto you, That whosoever shall say unto this mountain, Be thou removed, and be thou cast into the sea; and shall not doubt in his heart, but shall believe that those things which HE SAITH SHALL COME TO PASS; he SHALL have them." Isaiah 41:10 says, "Fear thou not; for I am with thee; be not dismayed; for I am thy God: I will STRENGTHEN thee; yea, I will help thee; yea, I will uphold thee with the right hand of my righteousness." Or Isaiah 41:13, which declares, "For I the LORD thy God will hold thy RIGHT HAND, saying unto thee, Fear not; I will help thee."

Such great reminders, though it's not always easy to recall during trying moments. This is why we must allow the Holy Spirit to bring ALL THINGS to our remembrance (See John 14:26). If you're still wondering WHY you're in your waiting season, just remember God knows the timing. Most importantly, He knows what you and I NEED! Why? Because you can't have JUST ANYONE!

CHAPTER 11:

The Best Is Yet To Come!

This chapter title is prophetic within itself. Why, might you ask? Because I truly believe the Lord dropped it in my spirit. You see, I thought I was going to end this book with chapter 10. But after finishing, I heard, "The best is yet to come..." As I wrote it down, I knew this was another chapter I would write.

Anticipation can leave us in suspense at times, because we don't know what's going to happen. To be honest, IT'S BEST that we don't know every step or move God will make in our lives. Why? Because if you're like me, you'll over-analyze. Two, it's so HE ALONE can be glorified!

What do you mean? When you know every step or move being made, not much trust is needed because you feel as though you know the outcome. (Not much is anticipated!) But when it comes to what GOD WANTS to orchestrate in our lives, it's like putting a blindfold on, unable to see or detect what's next. Hebrews 11:1 declares, "Now faith is the substance of things hoped for, the evidence of things NOT SEEN." You just have to trust Jesus and follow His every instruction. Knowing He's going to lead you in the right direction, without harm. This is where FAITH comes in!

Anticipation is a feeling of excitement about something that's GOING to happen. The ACT of preparing for something. Though you don't know what it is, our Father DOES! Have you ever felt last on the list for a SPECIFIC blessing? A particular breakthrough? Seemingly everyone is moving ahead, but you. They're celebrating while we're thinking, "What about me?" Two women of God last year in 2020, expressed to me as they were praying and prophesying that it's almost as if they heard me saying, "What about me?"

The Lord is blessing every other area. However, in this DISTINCT petition, He decides the time is not yet. What is this petition, you might ask? Marriage! Perhaps He wants to make this moment BIG! Like a grand finale!

We always hear the term, "Last, but certainly NOT least." What does this imply to me? Just because I'm last on the list doesn't mean I'm considered the least. I truly do believe good things come to those who WAIT! Habakkuk 2:2-3 declares, "And the LORD ANSWERED ME, and said, Write the vision and MAKE IT PLAIN upon tables, that he may run that readeth it. For the vision is yet for AN APPOINTED TIME, BUT AT THE END IT SHALL SPEAK, and not lie: though it tarry, WAIT FOR IT; because IT WILL SURELY COME, it will not tarry."

Single mothers, this Scripture should be inspirational for MANY of us that have heard the Father speak words of a surety over us! (You might need to read this Scripture a few times so that the Lord can speak to you concerning it. You may get a different revelation!) I got excited as I was typing it out! Philippians 4:6 also declares, "Be careful for nothing; but in everything by PRAYER and SUPPLICATION WITH THANKSGIVING let your requests be made known unto God."

Let us NOT STOP contending for what we are believing the Lord for! I know many of us are tired and might be saying, "I'm done!" Or "Whatever happens, happens!" But right at the end, when you've had enough, there's a breakthrough! The best IS YET to come, and you're right at the door! (I'm prophesying to myself!) I CAN'T QUIT!

Listen, when in labor and the baby's head is crowning, it hurts! Mommy has to BARE DOWN and endures the pain. But once the head comes through, the crowning is over, and the unbearable pain has reached its end. The blessing has arrived! ("The rest is history") She's able to hold her bundle of joy!

So likewise, with what you've prayed. There may have been some obstacles, hardships, and delays to what you've been asking from the Lord. You've cried, and doors have seemingly been shut in your face. Perhaps the Lord seems untraceable, or maybe you didn't receive an answer right then. It wasn't what you wanted to hear. But just like the Lord dropped it in my spirit, I say it to you. "The Best Is Yet To Come!" (Just like I heard it!)

Sometimes it seems too much to bear when you've seemingly had repeated cycles. There's a song in my spirit by Hezekiah Walker called "How Much We Can Bear." His choir says, "Jesus, He knows... how much we can bear. He knows... how much.... we can bear!"

Maybe you're at a point where you're tired of not seeing the manifestation of the prophetic words spoken over your life. I understand well...God, please perform these prophetic words you've spoken years ago because my eyes haven't beheld it yet! Make it TANGIBLE! (Perceptible by touch... real!) However, if the prophecy came with a set of instructions, it's up to us to follow them, as the LORD gave it.

Have you ever felt your situation was exhausted to the max?! What do you mean Tréasa? SPENT! FRAZZLED! My mother put it the best way; she would say, "Runnin' on E!". Lol (Meaning running empty)

Running out of options? Not with Jesus present! I'm reminded of Sarai and Abram, whose names were changed to Sarah and Abraham. Faced with being barren and never thinking they would conceive, they had a visitation from three men in their old age. (It was the LORD speaking to them) I declare and decree visitation, in the name of Jesus, to your current situation! In the book of Genesis, chapter 18: 9-15, the Bible declares, "And they said unto him, Where is Sarah thy wife? And he said, Behold in the tent. And he said, I will certainly return unto thee according to the time of life; and, lo, Sarah thy wife SHALL have a son. And Sarah heard it in the tent door, which was behind him. Now Abraham and Sarah were old and well stricken in age; and it ceased to be with Sarah after the manner of women. Therefore Sarah LAUGHED within herself, saying, After I am waxed old shall I have pleasure, my lord being old also? And the LORD said unto Abraham, Wherefore did Sarah laugh, saying, Shall I of a surety bear a child which am old? Is ANY THING too hard for the LORD? At the TIME APPOINTED I will return unto thee, according to the time of life, and Sarah SHALL HAVE a son. Then Sarah denied, saying, I laughed not; for she was afraid. And he said, Nay; `but thou didst laugh."

Similarly, in 2 Kings 4:15-17, Elisha calls for a Shunamite woman and tells her she will embrace a son, though her husband is old. It says, "And he said, CALL HER. And when he had called her, she stood in the door. And he said, ABOUT THIS SEASON according to the time of life, thou shalt embrace a son. And she said, Nay my lord, thou man of God, do not lie unto thine handmaid. And the woman CONCEIVED and bare a son at THAT SEASON that Elisha had said unto her, according to the time of life."

Like Sarah, it may seem laughable to us as well, for what we've been waiting a while for. Or like the Shunamite woman, we're speaking CONTRARY to that which God said amen. 2 Corinthians 1:20-21 declares, "For ALL the promises of God in him are yea, and in him Amen, unto the glory of God by us." It's one of those "Yeah, right" moments. I want to encourage us here!

Single mothers, as spoken in Sarah and Abraham's situation, I ask us now... Is anything too hard for the Lord? Do we truly believe in the appointed time God has for us in releasing a spouse or WHATEVER you've petitioned for? Is the timing of God frustrating us? I'll be honest, I've wondered why it's so difficult these days to get married. What's with this new age?

As mentioned in the previous chapter, there's a purpose BEYOND what our naked eye can see right now. Future hubby MUST line up with destiny and purpose! Let us wait for God's BEST! If we are honest, things got pretty ugly for us along the way. In the labor room, it's not pretty! The contractions a mother feels can feel like she's going to die! When will this be over? In our finite mind, for some of us, labor felt like an eternity! So likewise, our wait can feel lengthy.

Now maybe this is a bit exaggerated of an example when it comes to things that can wait. But many of us have been waiting 10 plus years, feeling like we're on edge and wondering what's wrong with us. Nothing is wrong; we just need to UNDERSTAND God's timing is perfect! Just like our bodies respond when it's time for the baby to come forth. Due to contractions, we know its delivery time. We're in ACTIVE LABOR! He knows WHEN to release the blessing! Isaiah 26:17 declares, "Like as a woman with child, that draweth near the time of her delivery, is in pain, and crieth out in her pangs; so have we been in thy sight, O LORD. Sure, God is working on us while we wait. In fact, we'll ALWAYS be working on something until we are called home to be with the Lord.

Ever wonder why people say, "I saved the best for last?" Perhaps they want to make this particular thing memorable, impactful! It's not just anything, but something of value. Something worth SEEING! This is not to say to those that received their blessing already, were not of importance, or didn't receive their best. It indicates there's a remnant of us that will be NEXT!

We've watched others receive theirs. In fact, we celebrated and rejoiced with them! I'm declaring and decreeing in this book that our waiting season is about to be over! With the Lord's perfect timing, it'll be our time to rejoice for what the Lord is doing for us! (Do we believe that?) Get ready! Our BEST is yet to come!

About The Author

Prophetess Tréasa Brown was born and raised in Boulder, Colorado. She's the 3rd child of 4 children and was dedicated back to the Lord as a child. Prophetess Brown was raised in the fear and admonition of the Lord and is a God-fearing woman as a result. The Lord saved her in January of 2012, and she was filled with the Holy Ghost, March 28th of 2012. Prophetess Brown was baptized in April of 2016 under Brian Carn Ministries and that same year, baptized by her former Pastor, Superintendent Charles E. Scurles. Prophetess Brown once served as a secretary in the

Young Women's Christian Counsel. She was a Primary Sunday School Teacher, Local District Sunshine Band Leader, Bible Band Teacher, Assistant Coordinator, for the Young Women of Excellence, a Praise and Worship Leader and has preached the Gospel. As a Leader, Prophetess Tréasa Brown is currently serving under the leadership of Pastor/Overseer Larry Herron and First Lady Herrron at Deliverance Jesus Is Coming Ministries. As a woman of God, she loves spending time in the presence of God and she is a prayer warrior and intercessor. Prayer is her passion! Prophetess Brown was destined to be a writer, an author. She has currently written two books by the instruction of Almighty God and Co-Authored a book with Prophetess Kimberly Moses titled, "I Almost Died." She's been an undercover journalist for nine years, writing prophetically while hearing, learning and studying the voice of God. Prophetess Brown enjoys encouraging others and is drawn to the brokenhearted. The Lord has called her to the nations, the prophetic ministry and to the office of the prophet. Prophetess Brown is yet to be birthed in the healing and deliverance ministry and the Lord is raising her up for His Glory! She has a hunger and a thirst for the things of God and her desire is to please the Father so He will get the Glory out of her life! She's excited about what He's going to do, as her ministry is born. To God Be The Glory!

Index

A

Abraham, 64, 65, 66, 87, 88
Abram, 87
ACTIVE LABOR, 89
Adam, 31
adolescence, 19
adulthood, 19
adventure, 65
affection, 51
afraid, 87
agony, 19
altar, 33
angry, 27

anointing, 49, 77, 78
Apostle WisePreach, 5, 36
apparel, 47
application, 3
APPOINTED, 24, 65, 84, 87
ashamed, 64
assignment, 13, 44, 48, 75
assistance, 3
attitude, 28
aunts, 1
author, 6, 15, 92

B

basket, 75
bat, 44
battle, 72
believe, 4, 7, 18, 19, 32, 35, 60, 62, 75, 77, 78, 80, 82, 84, 88, 90
believer, 27, 45, 60
benefits, 28, 62, 63
Bible, 5, 11, 12, 17, 23, 24, 25, 27, 40, 41, 44, 47, 54, 62, 70, 87, 92
bills, 4
BITTER, 32

blessing, 7, 15, 16, 83, 84, 85, 89, 90
Blessings, 6
bloodline, 1
BLUEPRINT, 8
body, 17, 25, 49, 51
Body of Christ, 25, 62
book, 7, 33, 49, 61, 73, 75, 77, 78, 82, 87, 90, 92
boy, 18
boyfriend, 20
Brandon Johnson, 7
breakthrough, 2, 83, 85
breakthroughs, 79
business, 7, 69
businesses, 8

C

calculate, 4
calm, 27
Canaanites, 65
candy, 75
CAPACITY, 27
cautious, 19, 32
cell phone, 64
challenge, 8, 12, 49, 51

character, 28
Cherith, 9
child, 3, 18, 19, 20, 87, 89, 91
children, 2, 3, 5, 11, 16, 17, 18, 19, 20, 21, 42, 61, 74, 91
Christ, 12, 17, 31, 33, 45, 51, 62, 74
church, 17, 22
circumstances, 3
Clark Sisters, 44
cliche, 69
cliff, 79
climax, 79
Cocoa Puffs, 5
Cohabitation, 62
Colorado, 60, 61, 62, 91
comfort zone, 27
Comforter, 41
communication, 26
conceal, 53
CONCEIVED, 88
confirmation, 36
confused, 50
conqueror, 69
conquerors, 68
consequences, 42, 60

Content and Records Department, 4
contract, 7
contractions, 89
controversial, 64
conversation, 34
conviction, 59, 63
COVID-19, 4, 8
cried, 20, 63, 85
crowning, 85
curses, 2
cycle, 1, 39, 70

D

dad, 17, 18
damage, 29
dangerous, 61
data, 2
dating, 62, 71
daughter, 35, 56, 63, 73
David, 30, 31
deceitful, 29, 49
decisions, 3, 42
dedication, 27
delay, 27, 79

deliverance, 33, 34, 35, 36, 37, 92
DELIVERANCE, 26
desert, 54
desk, 7
Desperation, 61
destiny, 43, 75, 77, 89
DESTINY, 8
DEVICES, 44
devil, 6, 44
die, 10, 51, 89
diligence, 70
disappointment, 68
disaster, 61, 79
discern, 50, 54, 57
discernment, 70
disciples, 11
discipline, 27
discouraged, 14
dismayed, 80
distraction, 35
DIVINE instructions, 6
divorce, 20, 69
domino effect, 19
door, 85, 87, 88
dormant, 30

DOUBLE MINDED, 40
doubt, 80

E

EBT, 2
emotions, 18, 33, 34, 42, 71
encourage, 13, 14, 16, 37, 49, 88
Ephesus, 22
error, 17, 29
Esther, 47, 48
eternity, 89
events, 33, 40
exam, 43
excellent, 73
expose, 37
exposure, 37

F

failures, 72, 79
faith, 7, 10, 15, 28, 43, 74, 78, 83
FAITH, 5, 10, 40, 83
faithful, 21
father, 17, 18, 19, 20, 57, 63

Father, 17, 25, 30, 41, 45, 49, 50, 62, 63, 71, 72, 74, 75, 83, 84, 92
Father's Day, 17
fear, 6, 61, 91
feelings, 42
finances, 6, 7
finger, 45
FIRST LOVE, 22
flesh, 9, 24, 26, 50, 51, 52, 60, 63
flight, 61
food stamps, 2, 3
fruit, 6, 27
FRUIT of the Spirit, 27
frustrated, 57
future, 2, 8, 13, 14, 16, 17, 19, 34, 43, 58, 63, 64, 70, 74

G

generations, 1
gentleness, 27
Gideon, 75, 76, 77
gift, 16, 71
giver, 12
Glory of the Lord, 36

God, 4, 5, 7, 8, 10, 12, 13, 14, 16, 17, 18, 20, 21, 22, 23, 24, 26, 27, 28, 29, 30, 33, 34, 36, 37, 40, 42, 43, 44, 45, 46, 48, 49, 50, 51, 52, 53, 54, 55, 56, 57, 58, 59, 60, 63, 64, 65, 66, 68, 69, 71, 73, 74, 75, 77, 78, 79, 80, 83, 85, 86, 88, 89, 91, 92, 93

goodness, 2, 28, 36

government, 3, 4, 12

government assistance, 3

grace, 48, 52

graceful, 37

grandparents, 1

GREAT COMMANDMENT, 23

growth, 26, 40, 46, 50, 52, 69

H

Haggai, 19

Hallelujah, 37

handsome, 31

hardships, 85

harsh, 72

healing, 19, 20, 33, 34, 92

health, 77

healthy, 32, 37

heartbreak, 69, 70, 71

heartbreaking, 68
hearts, 29, 30, 33
heavenly language, 63
HELP, 79
Hezekiah Walker, 86
high school, 14, 17, 58
hindrances, 43
history, 2, 85
Holy Ghost, 41, 50, 69, 91
HOLY GHOST, 25
Holy Spirit, 25, 63, 80
hook up, 75
hope, 28, 66, 79
hubby, 25, 74, 89
humans, 69
humble, 44
hurt, 19, 68, 71
husband, 13, 17, 25, 61, 62, 63, 64, 74, 88

I

identity, 25, 49, 54
IMPERATIVE, 22
improve, 36
improvement, 26

income, 8, 12
infertile, 41
infidelity, 69
inheritance, 2
iniquity, 30
innocence, 16, 21
INSANITY, 40
inspirational, 84
instructions, 27, 34, 64, 72, 86
interviewer, 3
Intimacy, 25
investment, 6
IRS, 5
ISSAC, 65
issue, 37, 70

J

Jesus, 2, 6, 8, 11, 12, 15, 20, 22, 23, 26, 27, 30, 31, 32, 33, 34, 37, 41, 44, 50, 53, 54, 69, 70, 72, 74, 79, 80, 83, 86, 87, 92
jewelry, 47
Jordan, 9
journey, 66, 70, 79
joy, 27, 45, 85

K

Kingdom of God, 5, 6
knees, 76

L

ladies, 42, 49, 52, 66, 78
laughed, 87
lesson, 40, 41, 42
liar, 6
longsuffering, 27
Lord, 3, 4, 5, 6, 7, 9, 10, 11, 12, 13, 14, 15, 16, 17, 18, 19, 21, 22, 23, 24, 25, 26, 27, 28, 30, 31, 33, 34, 35, 36, 37, 40, 42, 45, 48, 49, 51, 52, 53, 54, 55, 56, 57, 60, 61, 62, 64, 65, 66, 67, 69, 70, 71, 72, 73, 74, 75, 77, 78, 79, 82, 84, 85, 86, 88, 90, 91, 92
love, 18, 23, 27, 50, 56, 71

M

made-up mind, 27
maidservant, 44
makeover, 35

makeup, 47
malnourishment, 50
man, 2, 12, 18, 31, 32, 40, 46, 47, 50, 51, 60, 61, 62, 64, 66, 71, 75, 77, 88
marriage, 19, 24, 45, 69, 78, 79
married, 17, 20, 24, 25, 62, 78, 79, 89
Master, 14, 37
maturity, 40, 52
Medicaid, 2
memorable, 90
men of God, 5
mentality, 2
Midianites, 75, 76, 77
mildness, 27
miles, 54
mind, 23, 28, 32, 33, 35, 54, 61, 70, 75, 80, 89
MIND, 23, 49
ministry, 24, 49, 58, 92, 93
mistakes, 72
misunderstandings, 19
moderation, 27
mom, 17, 18, 20
Mommy, 85
money, 8, 11
motherhood, 16

mountain, 79, 80
mouth, 30, 31, 32, 33, 76
multiplication, 6

N

NECESSARY, 38
nervous, 36
new age, 89
newborn baby, 50
November, 35
nurture, 18, 49
nutritional diet, 47

O

obedience, 7, 27
Obedience, 27
obstacles, 85
offering, 12, 74
office, 5, 92
optimistic, 41
optimum, 73
out of order, 60

P

pain, 30, 56, 68, 85, 89
pandemic, 4, 15, 34
parents, 1, 17
Pastor Leech, 57
patience, 24, 27, 28, 74
peace, 27, 66
perception, 32
perfume, 47
PERIOD, 78
pitcher, 65, 66
PLAN, 16
pleasant, 37
pleasure, 3, 19, 87
potter's wheel, 57
poverty, 1, 2, 7
prayer, 2, 26, 49, 72, 92
prayer life, 26, 49
pregnant, 20
presence, 30, 36, 92
price tag, 67
procrastination, 6
promises, 88
prophecy, 6, 74, 86

prophesy, 6, 42, 57
Prophet Cedric Stanton, 5, 13
Prophet Cedric Wright II, 56
Prophet Elijah, 9
Prophet Fred Louis, 5
Prophetess Danielle Jean, 55
Prophetess Kimberly Moses, 7, 92
Prophetess Teneen Gainey, 56
prophetic call, 53
prophetic message, 35
PROVIDER, 3, 4
prudence, 27
purging, 33
purification, 35, 36
purpose, 75, 77, 78, 89
puzzle piece, 61

Q

quality, 73
queasy, 36

R

rain, 9, 79

raise, 18
raped, 20
reality, 19
rebuild, 35
reciprocation, 71
recondition, 36
reconstruct, 35
reconstruction, 30
red flags, 59, 64
Redeemer, 18
redesign, 36
re-equip, 35
refurbish, 36
rejection, 71
relationship, 25, 26, 34, 45, 49, 62, 69, 71
remembrance, 41, 80
remodel, 36
renew, 36
renovate, 35
REPENT, 19
repetitious cycles, 68
requests, 85
requirement, 22, 26
resources, 4, 8
resuscitate, 72

REVAMP, 35
revelation, 84
righteous, 20
righteousness, 5, 80
ring, 20
root, 33, 37

S

sacrifice, 27
Samuel, 27, 31
SANCTIFIED, 74
sanctified saints, 74
Sarah, 87, 88
Sarai, 87
school, 39
Scripture, 23, 42, 43, 51, 66, 80, 84
season, 4, 14, 22, 24, 39, 53, 54, 55, 56, 57, 80, 90
secret, 53
seed, 9, 19
selfish, 4, 19
semester, 39
setbacks, 79
sex, 60
Shunamite woman, 88

sin, 30, 31, 74
single Christian mother, 19
single ladies, 16
single mothers, 2, 10, 13, 17, 58, 66, 72
Single Mothers and Living for Christ, 7, 49, 61, 92
SINGLENESS SEASON, 24
smart, 6
SNAP, 2
society, 8, 29, 62
Son, 25, 30, 50
souls, 27
SOURCE, 4, 8
spirit, 25, 26, 30, 32, 41, 42, 45, 55, 82, 86
spiritual death, 50
spiritual eye, 14
spiritual eyes, 52
spitting up, 36
spouse, 13, 34, 70, 74, 88
stagnant, 8, 41
stagnation, 6, 50
statistics, 2
STEPPING STONE, 72
stimulus check, 5
STRENGTH, 46
STRENGTHEN, 80

stress, 33
stronghold, 33, 35
strongholds, 2
struggles, 1
success, 6, 70
sunshine, 79
surrender, 23
SUSTAINER, 4
symptoms, 5

T

TANF, 2
TANGIBLE, 14, 86
taste buds, 75
taxes, 5
teach, 18, 30, 41, 42
teacher, 41
tears, 20, 21
temperance, 27, 28
territory, 62
test, 10, 39, 41, 43, 45, 46
testimonies, 60, 69
text messages, 64
THANKSGIVING, 85

thoughts, 6, 70
time, 3, 7, 8, 15, 16, 18, 24, 25, 30, 32, 34, 41, 44, 49, 52, 53, 54, 55, 58, 69, 71, 72, 78, 79, 84, 87, 88, 89, 90, 92
toiletries, 4
tolerance, 27
tongues, 63
Tony Brown, 49
tragedy, 79
train, 18
transgression, 31
Tréasa Brown, 37, 73, 91, 92
treasure, 58
TREASURE, 14
treasury, 11
trial, 45
trouble, 27, 63
trust, 14, 44, 75, 78, 83
truth, 42, 66, 77

U

unbearable, 70, 85
uncles, 1
unconditional love, 71

UNDERSTANDING, 40
unemployed, 8
UNMARRIED, 24, 25
unproductive, 41, 54
unrevealed, 53
update, 35
uproar, 34
upset, 27
USA Facts, 2

V

veiled, 53
verbalized, 30, 33
victories, 79
videos, 60
vigilant, 44
vipers, 30
virgins, 48
vision, 49, 56, 84
visitation, 87
voice of God, 26, 59, 92
vomit, 36

W

warfare, 63
water, 10, 56, 65, 66, 76, 77
wealth, 2, 3, 5
Welfare, 1, 3, 15
wicked, 29
wickedness, 30
widow, 10, 11
wife, 17, 25, 64, 65, 87
WIFE, 24
wilderness, 53, 54, 57
willingness, 27
wisdom, 18, 40, 44, 45, 61
women of God, 3, 77, 78, 83
world, 8, 14, 24, 25, 30, 31, 50, 51
worshiped, 66

Y

young lady, 16, 59
YouTube, 36, 55, 60

Z

Zarephath, 9

www.ingramcontent.com/pod-product-compliance
Lightning Source LLC
Chambersburg PA
CBHW072037110526
44592CB00012B/1458